RELATIONSHIP BOOK FOR WOMEN

QUEEN OF HEARTS

Become The Woman You Were Always Meant To Be

Susan Doyle

Table of Contents

PART 1 5
Chapter 1: 7 Signs Of True Love 6
Chapter 2: 7 Signs Someone Will Be Your Best Friend for Life. 11
Chapter 3: 7 Ways to Keep Your Relationship Fresh and Exciting 16
Chapter 4: 7 Ways To Achieve Harmony In Personal Relationships 20
Chapter 5: 6 Ways To Stay Committed In A Relationship 24
Chapter 6: 6 Signs You're Unsure Of Your Level of Commitment 28
Chapter 7: 6 Signs of An Incompatible Relationship 32
Chapter 8: 6 Ways To Have A Great First Date 37
PART 2 42
Chapter 1: 6 Ways To Deal With Manipulative Partners 43
Chapter 2: 7 Ways to Deal With Sexual Problems In A Relationship ...48
Chapter 3: 7 Signs You Are Falling Out of Love 52
Chapter 4: 7 Signs You Cannot Handle A Relationship 57
Chapter 5: 7 Signs That You Were Never In Love 63
Chapter 6: 7 Ways To Be More Mature In A Relationship 68
Chapter 7: 7 Ways to Keep Your Relationship Fresh 72
PART 3 77
Chapter 1: 7 Signs you're More Attractive Than You Think 78
Chapter 2: 7 Ways To Deal With Growing Apart In A Relationship 83
Chapter 3: 7 Signs You've Outgrown Your Friendship 87
Chapter 4: 6 Signs You Need To Give Yourself Some Personal Space.92
Chapter 5: 7 Signs You're Becoming Toxic 96
Chapter 6: 7 Signs That You're Ready To Take Your Relationship To The Next Level 101
Chapter 7: 6 Signs You Need To Give Your Partner Some Space 106
Chapter 8: 5 Steps To Use Dating Apps Correctly 110
Chapter 9: 7 Ways To Become A Good Partner 114

PART 1

Chapter 1:
7 Signs Of True Love

True love! The words themselves carry too much weight. It's so hard to find true love nowadays and even harder to keep it. You have to walk not only on the rose petals but the thorns too. You have to suffer from many wrong partners to get the right one finally, and even then, you might be unsure if they're the one for you. The feeling of warmth, passion, and desire, the unconditional sentiment, irrespective of good times or bad, everyone seems to want that.

It is truly a fantastic experience. True love should be effortless and absolute. It should defy all established logic of human behavior. The honeymoon phase is, no doubt, the best position you find yourself and your partner in. You wish that you could be stuck in this phase forever. But when the sparks settle and the bursts of infatuation start to fade, and you find yourself noticing their flaws, having arguments and misunderstandings with them, or simply seeing their imperfections, you begin to enter into the real picture. This is when most couples drift apart. But if the arguments make your relationship stronger and you find yourself coming back to this person, then you've indeed found your true love.

While true love may be indescribable, there are ways to know what really is true love and what characteristics and factors contribute to true love.

Here are 7 Signs you should look out for:

1. True Love is Selfless

It is like humans to expect something in return when you put your efforts, time, and energy into a person. And if they don't reciprocate it back, you find yourself being distant and detached from the person. But that's not the case with someone you genuinely love. You give yourself wholeheartedly to that person because you want to and do not expect anything in return. There is no anticipation of a reward. The good thing is, your partner would repay you with his time, sleep, company, and with everything that will make you happy, all on his own, without you even asking anything from him. He would make sure to appreciate you and make small gestures to realize your worth in his life.

2. You Both Are Open To Change

Love is all about accepting each other's flaws and imperfections. But it is also the most transformative power on the Earth. Whether it's following a specific diet to look good for them, buying new outfits, working on your insecurities and weaknesses, or listening to their point of view respectfully even though you're murdering them in your head, it's all about the internal self-growth and becoming a better person for them. Talking to your partner about something he did that bothered you and him apologizing to you instead of being rude and promising you that he will work on himself is clearly a sign of true love.

3. Your Family And Friends Are In The Know

One of the indications of true love is that both your family and friends know about the other. Your partner genuinely wants to meet them and has the desire to be accepted by them. Your family and friends, too, have approved of him and want you to cling to that person forever. His closed ones have made your visits easier by making you comfortable and relaxed around them, and they, too, have approved of you. This acceptance cannot be understated. Whilst it is your decision to make at the end of the day, this confirmation from family and friends only serve to strengthen the belief you have inside that this person is the right one for you. It is not everything but it is a huge step forward.

4. No Need To Hide Anything

When you're in love, you immediately want to tell your partner all about your day and give them all the news instantly, no matter how good or bad it is. You both share your lives openly with each other and you don't feel the need to hide anything from them. If you sincerely and honestly talk about your insecurities or the things that make you feel bad and get reassurance from your partner in return, then you've indeed found the one. True love is all about being vulnerable and expressing your true self to your partner without the fear of what he might think.

5. You take care of each other's needs.

From washing the dishes when they're tired to taking care of their laundry when they've forgotten, or making their favorite food when they're hungry and giving them their medicines on time when they're sick, you both make sure that you're taking care of the other person when they need it. You also make small gestures like preparing a date for them or sending them flowers or notes, just to remind them that they're on your mind and having to see that cute smile on their face. The element of surprise never ceases to amaze your partner.

6. Looking towards the future.

If you imagine your future, say, 10 or 20 years from now, and the idea of not being with your current partner makes your eye all watery, and your heart starts aching but imagining them with you in your future make you all mushy and happy, then you have found the true love of your life. You both talk about your plans and commit to each other because you both find yourself compatible with each other, knowing that you both can't live without each other. We only want to think ahead if we believe there is something there to look forward to, otherwise it all just seems like one giant blur to us.

7. You avoid hurting each other in any way.

True love is all about making sacrifices for your partner and making their happiness a priority (this, in no way, means that your happiness doesn't matter, it should always be on top of the list). But avoiding arguments and conflicts or resolving them respectfully is essential. Even if you do hurt your partner, apologizing to them straight away and making up to them by doing their favorite things counts a lot.

Conclusion:

Love isn't about setting up high expectations or traps for your partner; neither is it about hitting some perceived societal goals. It is about finding someone who understands you, wants the same things as you do, and wants to build a future together with you. It should be supportive, fulfilling, and patient. It's not always about the grand gestures or dramatic displays of passion, but something that feels natural and effortless. And if you do find someone with who you share this beautiful experience, fight for them and never let them go.

Chapter 2:
7 Signs Someone Will Be Your Best Friend for Life.

Blood may be thicker than water, but a good friend can become as important as a family in no time. We might often ask ourselves this question, what would we ever do without our best friend? They just make everything so easier and better. Celebration card specialists Hallmark conducted a poll of 2000 adults, asking them about their best friends. A massive 84% of the group believed that a true best friend is someone you can go weeks or even months without seeing, but it's like nothing has ever changed when you meet them.

There are people we considered our dearest but somehow drifted apart from them. Yet, while there are those, we have managed to keep in our lives forever, no matter what it takes. These are the ones who show up on our doorstep with ice cream and DVDs when we're going through some crisis, who knows us inside and out, with whom we share our inside jokes and texts them instantly whenever we have any exciting news or any minor inconvenience happens. They're the ones who will stand by us and will fight for us when the world turns against us.

If you're looking for some signs to help you identify your current best friend, then say no more!

Here are 7 ways to know if someone will be your best friend for life:

1. You compliment each other's personalities:

Sometimes, you meet a person and click with them instantly. Everything feels easier with them. You start to notice that although both of Ya'll personalities may be different, and they somehow align together. You balance out each other weaknesses and strengths without clashing too much. You may have a difference of opinion and views with them, but you both respect each other and agree to disagree. You may be the adventurous and aggressive type while your friend may be the calm and level-headed type, but you both get along ideally. It would help if you had someone like them in your life who will give you peace and comfort, while they need someone like you in theirs who will stand up for them.

2. The friendship seems effortless:

A lot of times, no matter what the relationship is, they demand efforts and hard work. But when you're with your best friend, you feel like the friendship is flowing smoothly and effortlessly. You don't have to cling to them every day and remind them of your presence. Both of you know that you will be there for each other in times of need. You feel emotionally recharged after meeting them instead of being exhausted and drained out. They keep a check on you from time to time, and you do that too. You don't need to pretend to be someone else when you're with them. Both of you are your true, genuine, vulnerable self with each other.

3. **They know you too well:**

Even if you both have just met some months or years ago, there is an instant deep connection that you know each other for decades. They can tell that something is bothering you by looking at your facial expressions or the different tones in your texts. They understand what goals and dreams you have been working hard for, and they support you wholeheartedly. They know about your daily routine, your little quirks, what makes you happy, and what annoys you; they just get you in a way no one ever has. They uplift your upset mood by sending you your favorite chocolates or making you your favorite food. They make an effort to show you how well appreciated and well deserved you are in their eyes.

4. **You trust them with your life:**

The essential foundation of any relationship is trust. It just doesn't come off as a reward, but instead, you have to prove yourself worthy, gain and protect it with all your heart and soul. A best friend is someone you can tell every good and bad to, without any second thoughts. You know well that they won't judge you, even if you show them your darkest parts. So you always have your best friend on the speed dial, listed as an emergency contact, and text and call them right away whenever something happens. You don't doubt even a fraction of their loyalty and knows that they won't ever take advantage of you, abandon you, or betray you.

5. **You treat them like family:**

Just like we can't imagine our life without our family, we indeed can't imagine it without our friends too. You invite them over for special occasions or events or family holidays, and they participate just the same as your family members. Your parents treat them like their own child; they've become great friends with your siblings and pets, and even your relatives too. They treat your house like their own and are comfortable enough to show up uninvited.

6. **They make you feel motivated:**

A best friend is someone who makes sure that you become a better version of yourself every day. You look up to them for inspiration, and they motivate you to be a better person and do better in life. They don't point out your flaws and weaknesses and joke about your insecurities. Instead, they help you to overcome your bad phases and become your biggest cheerleader. Maybe you've seen them struggling too, but they still manage to wear that bright and beautiful smile whenever they are with you. This makes you adore and admire them and get motivated by them. Even though you know all the dark parts of each other, the mutual respect and the chance to help each other grow are still there.

7. You're honest with each other and are willing to work it out:

It sometimes happens that both of you end up hurting each other, either intentionally or unintentionally. You may feel awkward to bring it to their attention that they've caused you pain. But communication is the key to any relationship. The importance of talking and sorting out whatever's hurting you or them is essential if you want to keep each other in your lives. Conflict is also an opportunity to learn more about the other person, and it also helps us grow. But despite your arguments and fights, you both work it out, apologize to each other, and avoid hurting each other again. You both know that the true essence of friendship is maintaining it, despite the good or bad that happens.

Conclusion:

At the end of the day, we enjoy being with people who make our life easier, not complicate it—the people who get us and make the world a better place for us. No matter how serious life gets, we always need someone we can be our stupid selves with. If these signs match the person that you are thinking about, make sure that you cling on to them and not let them go. Life is hard enough as it is, we should be with people that we can walk through life together through the thick and thin with.

Chapter 3:
7 Ways to Keep Your Relationship Fresh and Exciting

At the beginning of a relationship, one can feel the excitement and the sparks that come from the newness of a relationship. For example, the butterflies you feel before going on a date can make you feel surprisingly on top of the world. It is the start of a relationship that makes you feel this way. At the beginning of a relationship, everything feels fresh as your partner surprises you and makes you feel special.

But as time goes on, the relationship becomes boring. This can often lead to an end of a relationship; to prevent this, you could always keep your relationship fresh and exciting. Even though now both of you are not the same person you used to be in each other's eyes, but you could still maintain that tingly sensation by trying to be more surprising.

Here are seven ways to keep your relationship fresh and exciting.

1. Keep Surprising Each Other

At the start of every relationship, partners often surprise each other with flowers, gifts, or a surprise date. These surprises cause the other partner to feel beloved. Still, people usually stop surprising their partners with such things as time goes on. By continuing to surprise your partner with gifts, flowers, and sweet notes, you keep your relationship fresh. After a while, you learn about the likes and dislikes of your partner. You can easily use that to your advantage by buying them flowers they like or small presents that make them happy. The happiness caused by these small gestures of love can keep the relationship from becoming dull. So don't let the element of surprise die.

2. Ask Them Out On A Date

A relationship often begins with a date, and the date makes you feel nervous and excited. Meeting your partner for the first few times can make you want to look the best version of yourself and continue your efforts to look and be the best for your partners. So don't stop the efforts. Ask your partner out on a fancy date to make them happy. Even if you are just ordering food from outside, you could still light up some candles and set the table with a fancy dinner set. This could make your partner feel special, and the freshness of the relationship doesn't die with time.

3. Try Something New Together

Always try to do something new, like watching movies you liked as a teenager or eating something you haven't tried before; it awakes the excitement your partner feels throughout the day. Try going ice skating or skateboarding together as a fun activity, taking time from your adult routine, and going hiking and other activities to have fun together simply.

4. Speak About Your Feelings Towards Them

Try voicing your thoughts about them. Don't shy away from words and tell them or remind them regularly how much they mean to you or how strongly you feel towards them; simple sentences like "I love you" can profoundly affect your partner. Please don't take your partner for granted but make them feel good about themselves and tell them how important they are in your life. This can make them appreciate your presence, and the relationship will remain fresh.

5. Set Life Goals Together

You and your partner can decide on some goals that you can achieve together as a couple. It can be any goal, as a financial goal, or exploring the world together. You could save money for vacations together. During this journey, you can motivate each other but can still have fun. Moreover, when you work as a team, it will also strengthen your bond.

6. Turn Off Your Phone

When spending time with each other, try turning off your phone. This will show your partner how important they are to you. Focus on their words and respond actively. Studies show that a relationship can end when you are more focused on social media apps than on your partner. Using too many social media apps can distance you from your partner; try spending more time with them than using your mobile phone and reestablish your bond with them.

7. Greet Each Other With Excitement

When a relationship begins, we often see couples embracing each other with love and passion even when they met just yesterday. Still, as time passes, couples can be seen greeting each other with just a simple hello or a short hug. Greeting your partner with excitement and enthusiasm can make them long to meet you. They would be excited all day long because of the way you greet them. This can ensure that the excitement of the relationship doesn't die. You can greet them with a warm, comforting hug or simply a few exciting words; saying mushy things can also make them feel loved, like "I missed you" when they come back home from work.

By following the above ways, you can keep your partner happy and your relationship fresh and exciting.

Chapter 4:
7 Ways To Achieve Harmony In Personal Relationships

How beautiful the world or life would be if we were all blessed with harmonious relationships. The kind that is selfless, giving, and nurturing, the kind that doesn't have any tussle of egos and power play. Just you and your significant other fitted together, like a hand in the glove. Harmony isn't an inherent trait; that is one of the reasons why it becomes too difficult for relationships to flow seamlessly. Here are some tips and tricks to build a harmonious relationship with others.

1. Harmony Can Be Nurtured

Before getting into the ways to let go of all the negativities and build a holistic, harmonious relationship, we must first understand why harmonious relationships are essential. A harmonious person is defined as someone who is easygoing and has the ability to get along well with others. A harmonious bond is something that two people experience without fighting, clashes, or ego tussles. But most of the time, one of the partners might feel negative emotions, which can affect the quality of the relationship. Feeling discontent in a relationship might have distressing and overwhelming experiences, but that does not in any way means that we should lose all hope.

2. Be the best version of yourself:

If you look into your personal relationships to compensate for your loneliness, you are bound to get disappointed sooner or later. It indeed takes two to tango, but building a relationship and making sure it lasts has a lot to do with your state of mind. You have to be peaceful with yourself first before achieving peace in your personal relationships. Over-expecting things from your partners or others would always lead to disappointment, which will, in turn, channel into challenges and difficulties in your relationship. You have to be the bearer of harmony that you wish to cultivate in your relationships. You can start by fixing the broken things on your end, and others will eventually follow you.

3. Embrace acceptance:

Resistance and harmony can never go hand in hand. If you wish to achieve harmony, you have to let go of resisting the current order of things or change. Resistance can be in the form of criticizing your partner for whatever behaviors and traits they possess and forcing them to change who they are. This would lead to negativity and tension in the relationship. Going from resistance to acceptance is a passable road that will lead you towards building a harmonious relationship. You have to be aware that no one is perfect, even ourselves. We are bound to make mistakes and have flaws and have to accept others and their defects and errors.

4. Let go of the hurt and negativity:

Sometimes, it's our baggage of the past that keeps us unable to build a harmonious relationship. For example, it might be something that your ex-partner did to immensely hurt you, or a family member criticized you. However, you didn't process this hurt nor gave it the time to heal, but instead decided to bottle up your decisions and move on. It is only natural that the negative feelings you are keeping inside you for a long time will come out when someone bad triggers you. In this case, you have to find a way to let go of whatever hurt you're feeling, channel all your negativity, and foster harmony in your relationships.

5. Practice compassion:

You have to internalize gentleness and compassion, both as an individual and a couple if you want to build a close and harmonious relationship. When you address and approach any conflict and issue with gentleness, your mind will automatically respond with empathy rather than jumping to conclusions. This will facilitate open communication and inhibitions. It will also enable you to view the other person's perspective and views with kindness. This would put you in a position to give your partner space to process their thoughts and emotions.

6. Free yourself from expectations:

The stringent expectations we might feel from our loved ones can take a toll on our equation with them. While it is only natural to expect some things from the people we love, we shouldn't set them in stone. Because unmet expectations lead to a handful of negative emotions of disappointment, hurt, and anger, you end up saying hurtful things to other people. Instead of expecting too much, accept them as they are, allow them to be their own person, and appreciate the good they bring into the relationship. Appreciate their efforts even if they don't go your way.

7. **Give and seek space in your relationships:**

Personal space is one of the rarest yet one of the most crucial elements of feeling at peace in your relationships. Oftentimes, we get so much tethered with our loved ones that it feels like a permanent embrace. It may seem exciting and comforting at first, but soon it will leave you guys feeling suffocated from each other. We must understand that everyone needs their space t catch a breath, reflect, unwind and grow. It is also a hallmark of a healthy bond. To build a harmonious relationship, you must dismantle the clingy approach and give each other all the space you need.

Conclusion:

A harmonious relationship needs sustained efforts and nurturing, and you can neither expect to achieve harmony overnight nor do expect it to last forever once achieved. But it is sure is worth every effort. The importance of building a harmonious relationship lies in the fact that it brings you peace and hope, the two things most vital to any individual.

Chapter 5:
6 Ways To Stay Committed In A Relationship

Intro:

Once you and your partner decide to transition from a newly dating into a long-term committed relationship, you will experience some challenges and changes. A long term relationship will come with a lot of benefits. You will be closer to each other and also more comfortable in each other's presence. But it will also come with some difficulties, you will have to put in work, but you do not have to complicate it. You should focus on establishing healthy standards and habits that work for both of you. We are going to list 6 ways that will help you stay in a committed relationship.

1. **Communication:**

Now, this might not sound like a piece of revolutionary advice, but communication is a critical factor for a healthy, committed relationship. When your communication is based on honesty, the trust in your relationship will increase, and your partner will also feel supported and safe if you are prone to people-pleasing than deep, real, effective communication can be exhausting. But you can only have a healthy relationship if you voice your opinions and tell them what is bothering you. Good communication also means recognizing all the things you are grateful for in the relationship. After all, healthy communication is not always negative.

2. Engage in Self-Growth:

It is essential to focus on personal goals and self-growth even when you are in a relationship. Most people fall into the trap of investing most of their energy in the relationship and their partner, and they forget to prioritize their own needs and wants, which results in them feeling exhausted most of the time. To make a relationship healthy, it is essential to recognize your needs and then voice them. When you focus on actualizing your goals and self-care, you will feel more fulfilled, which will lead to you feeling more comfortable in your relationship.

3. Boundaries:

An essential part of relationships is boundaries. They can be emotional, sexual or physical. You need to set and communicate your boundaries with your partner in a committed relationship. When you have been together for a very long time, your partner might assume that some things are fine with you when in reality, they are not. At the beginning of the relationship, you let things slide because perhaps you did not have the confidence to talk about them or maybe your views on certain things have changed. Regardless it is important to set healthy boundaries so your relationship can flourish.

4. Focus on Intimacy:

Intimacy is much more than your sex life. The intimacy that will foster trust between you and your partner is physical and emotional closeness. Often when people are in long-term relationships, they forget the importance of intimacy. When you get comfortable around your partner, often you forget to show your love and affection. You might think it is silly of you to keep saying I love you over and over again. You have been together for a long time, and of course, they know it, but that is not the case; to have a healthy relationship, you need to remind your partner that you still care and matter to you.

5. Appreciate Your Differences:

You and your partner are two unique individuals with different perspectives, pasts, and destinations. You need to recognize this. Maybe these differences are what make you such a great couple. Even if you are not the opposite attracts kind of couple, you will have some differences that are the reason for friction in your relationship. You should never try to change your partner, whether there are some larger things you think need to change or small things that irritate you. You should accept them for who they are, with their differences for a healthy relationship.

6. Relish:

There can be times when your relationship goes awry, and you will need professional help to get back on track, and even if that is not the case, there can be times when you are just looking for advice to improve your relationship and make it more healthy. If you have found yourself in the same situation, you should consider downloading an app called "Relish". Relish is an app designed for relationship coaching. It can help you and your partner evaluate the current status of your relationship and help identify how you can improve your relationship. Professional coaches are available on relish, which can help you with different relationship struggles you are facing and put your relationship back on a healthy track.

Conclusion:

You need to have a healthy, long-lasting relationship, and we are sure these 6 ways will go a long way. With time a relationship can turn toxic, and there is no big deal in that you just have to know how you can fix that. Lastly, you should never forget about your personal growth and priorities and goals because that will satisfy you.

Chapter 6:
6 Signs You're Unsure Of Your Level of Commitment

Commitment phobia usually comes from the lack of clarity about what we want for ourselves. It is recurrent among the millennials these days. The definition of love has changed drastically over the years and is not just black and white anymore. Relationships often work if you are lucky enough. Still, you could also be one of those people who can't see themselves having a long-term committed relationship. If you think you aren't ready for a relationship, there's no need to blame yourself. But there are some pointers that you should heed.

Relationships aren't your typical movie where you get to dance your heart out with your lover while slow music plays in the background. It is more like becoming self-aware of the things you want and giving yourself bitter reality checks that could help you understand yourself better. Here are some signs that you might be unsure of your level of commitment.

1. **You Feel Insecure All The Time**

Being insecure in your relationship can prove as an obstacle in your level of commitment. You might be worried about the future all the time, afraid that your partner might leave you, or assume that it won't work out. The enormity of it all makes it difficult for you to step into a committed relationship. Insecurities can get diminished if you get ample amounts of validation. Still, they can also prove to be toxic at some point. Suppose you're constantly looking to fill a void inside you by people's validation. In that case, it means you're not ready to get yourself committed. Complete dependency can prove fatal in a relationship.

2. **You Have Unresolved Feelings**

This is one of the most crucial reasons why we can't commit to a relationship. Although such feelings are only a part of being human, we deny them and run from them rather than resolving them. Unless you find closure for yourself, there's no way you can work it out with someone else. You need to bite down and allow yourself to feel all the things that you were escaping from. You must follow your instincts and find a way to work out those ill feelings before they come stumbling all over your life and relationship.

3. **You're Waiting For The Right Person**

Maybe you have the right person all along, but you are taking them for granted? You can be an arrogant prick all you want, but taking the right person for granted will only do you more harm than good. Love isn't always about flowers and poetry; we have to become self-aware when looking for the right person. You must clear all your self-doubts and accept people with all of their imperfections. It won't be hard for you to find the right person unless you don't want things to work out.

4. You Have Major Commitment Issues

People lack the courage to admit this, but it cannot be trivialized. If you are in love with a person but can't commit to them, then the problem is in you and not in the relationship. Commitment is the first step that breaks the water down to its molecular level. It is the step that ensures you are not alone anymore. Suppose you can allow the person in your daily routine, and you're okay with them being around you. In that case, you will slowly learn to steer clear of commitment phobia.

5. You Want To Make Your Own Decisions

Your issues can be less emotional and external if you are not ready to be in a relationship but love with the person. Being in a relationship means you have to take care of certain decisions, from their likes and dislikes to even the tiniest things that can either make or ruin their day. You might be well used to being independent and resent any decision that your partner may take on behalf of both of you. Perhaps you still haven't learned how to let the reigns go and share them with somebody else, or you find it hard to picture sharing your responsibility with someone else.

6. You Are Looking For Perfection

This is something that you know in your heart that you will never find. But being in the constant bubble of finding someone perfect gives you the excuse to delay your relationship. The reality is that under the garb of looking for perfection, you are feeding your commitment phobia. Setting unrealistic standards and always looking for someone ideal won't get you anywhere when dating. You have to make sure that you accept the other person with all of their flaws, just as they welcome you with yours!

Conclusion

Being unsure of your level of commitment is okay, but dragging someone and confusing them with your feelings is not. You have to compromise unconditionally, so it doesn't haunt your conscience. If you have to commit, do it wholeheartedly. If not, be clear about it.

Chapter 7:
6 Signs of An Incompatible Relationship

You might have heard the word 'compatibility' a million times before starting a new relationship or even after getting into one. But what exactly does the word 'compatibility' means? Compatibility is when you and your partner not only share the same interests but also share the same values, goals, have compatible libidos, support each other in their times of distress and frustration, help them achieve their dreams, make each other feel safe, and plan a future where you can both see each other being together and happy. However, not every couple is blessed with the joys of having a compatible relationship. Melody Kiersz, a professional matchmaker, says, "There are some obvious ones, like not wanting the same things in life, lifestyle choices in terms of travel or location, and relationship style (I.e., monogamous vs. Polyamorous)."

No matter how much in love you are with your partner and how desperately you compromise in your relationship to make everything seem better, if you both aren't compatible, then the relationship might have a dead-end in the long run. Here are some signs that will help you see if you are in an incompatible relationship.

1. **Your partner doesn't respect the differences:**

There's rarely a time when you might feel that you have found a person just like you. People are different from each other. Sometimes, their passion or goals may align with yours, but some differences are always there. You may like to read a book or watch a movie in your free time instead of your partner playing a video game or going outdoor with their friends. If your partner doesn't respect the differences and forces you to change your hobbies and dreams, then it's a red flag. After all, respect is the critical element to any lasting relationship. In an incompatible relationship, your partner might make you feel bad about being different from them and may mock you about the different things you do.

2. **Your partner gets overly jealous:**

We, as human beings, cannot wholly eliminate the factor of jealousy from within ourselves. Being jealous and possessive of your partner isn't a bad thing, as long as you have it under control. But if your partner gets overly jealous of petty things, keeps a regular check on you and your whereabouts, and constantly bugs you, then it will not only make you frustrated, but you will eventually be exhausted, and your mental health will shamble. This isn't just a sign of incompatibility but also a sign of toxicity.

3. **You're a different version of yourself around them:**

What is a relationship if you don't even feel comfortable around your partner? Out of all the people, your love interest should be the one with whom you can be yourself and not pretend. You find yourself always pretending to be a perfect flawless creature because they might have said something or showed you that they wouldn't accept the things that your real version does. The constant struggle of making yourself look ideal in Infront of your partner's eyes would eventually drain you out. You might stop pretending after a while, and your partner may or may not like it. If your partner doesn't like the real you, then you should consider this as an incompatible relationship and move on.

4. Lack of communication:

A lasting relationship is based on communicating effectively with your partner. For example, suppose you feel like your partner discards your feelings and consider them stupid after you tell them that something's been bothering you or tells them that something they've said might have hurt you. In that case, your partner is being emotionally unavailable and doesn't value your feelings. As a result, you might feel uneasy about opening up to them, and they might feel the same about you. This is one of the significant reasons for the incompatibility between the partners. If you aren't ready to share your feelings with them or get ignored if you share them, the relationship will eventually come down the hill.

5. Your partner does not take care of your wants and needs:

Consider this, and you have just come home after a long day of work, hoping to get some rest. As soon as you arrive, there is a long pile of dishes waiting for you, and your partner tells you to make something for dinner. Yep, you can imagine the reaction your partner would get. A relationship should be based on mutual efforts and understanding. If your partner is doing the bare minimum and you find yourself putting in all the efforts, then you definitely don't deserve to be with a person like them. Instead, your partner should treat you special every now and then, makes you realize your worth in his life, takes care of you, and make small gestures to show his love.

6. Fighting gets ugly with them:

Arguing and fighting are the forte of every relationship. What matters is how you resolve the issue after you've argued or fought. In a compatible relationship, couples always try to sort out the things bothering them, and they eventually apologize to each other. While in an incompatible relationship, you would find your partner constantly bickering and mocking long after the fight has ended. You both won't see eye to eye with each other for days and may go to bed angry at each other. Your partner isn't open to change and doesn't respect your views and opinions. You can't agree to disagree with each other and tries to prove the other wrong no matter what. If you find yourself spending more time fighting with your partner than being happy, you clearly are mismatched.

7. Different outlooks on the future:

Two people may be in the same relationship, but they rarely are on the same page. While one might be thinking about getting engaged or married soon, the other might flee to the hills just at the mere name of commitment. One might talk about having kids one day while the other just brushes off the idea that they're not ready for that yet. One must be thinking about traveling the world while the other just wants to stay peacefully in the town. It's best to start talking about your future early in the relationship to see where both of you stand in each other's lives.

Conclusion:

The signs mentioned above are all the major red flags of incompatibility. But, in addition, you must have a sense of mutual respect, understanding, and effort with your partner. For example, suppose you feel that the relationship is one-sided, with you giving your all, making sacrifices, trying to be consistent with them. Yet, at the same time, they couldn't care less about you and don't appreciate or value all that you do for them. In that case, you should consider moving out of the relationship for good.

Chapter 8:
6 Ways To Have A Great First Date

Have you been crushing on someone hard for a long time and finally dared to ask them out? Well, congratulations that they've said yes! Or else why would you be here looking for ways to arrange a perfect date with them? Planning a good date can be nerve-wracking, especially if it's your first one and you have to make sure everything goes well and smoothly. You work hard on every detail so as to impress your date, and as the quote suggests, "the first impression is the last impression," you really are working on going the extra mile.

While you're hesitant that you need to plan a perfect date, you're also trying not to look too desperate or investing in something that may be won't work out. For example, if you have planned an expensive dinner in a luxurious restaurant but within minutes you realize that you don't click with your date, it will be pretty awkward for the both of you.

To help you with your anxieties, we have come up with some strategies and ways to make sure you have a great first date!

1. **Don't try to overcomplicate things:**

A first date is usually full of nervousness and uncertainty. There's a great chance that you know just a little about them, or maybe not at all. You have to make sure that you don't complicate things by making either very grand plans or keeping them to yourself for the whole day. Remember, you have to make them comfortable first, and these extravagant things definitely won't help with that. You can simply ask them out for a coffee or take them to watch a movie. This will help both you and your date decide if you want to spend more time with each other. If you both click well, a simple coffee in your local coffee shop will lead to lunch and dinner, or maybe more hangouts.

2. Get yourself into engaging conversations:

A personality would be rated 10/10 if the person has a deeper understanding and is intellectually clever. If you suffer from social anxiety or are quiet most of the time, you should prepare yourself with some intelligent topics beforehand to woo your date. Chances are, your date would most likely give you a poor score if you use cheesy pickup lines, lacking humor and empty compliments. It would be best if you tried telling an engaging story about your life that will impress your date instantly, and likewise, listen attentively to whatever the other person says about theirs. It would help if you practiced self-compassion before going, be confident enough that you're going to impress them. Having self-doubts and anxiety is expected before any significant event, but make sure it doesn't get to you.

3. Think about your past mistakes:

Have you been on several dates that ended up in disasters? And now you can't help but make sure this one doesn't end in the dumps too. For that, you have to use your power of memory flashbacks and relive every date you've been on. What was it that made your dates run away and not look back again? Maybe you weren't listening to them hard enough, or maybe your phone looked more of your date than the person sitting in Infront of you; perhaps you passed an unkind comment or hurt the other person's sentiments in some way, even if it was unintentional and you didn't realize it at that time. But it's okay. You should try and correct your mistakes instead of overthinking and dwelling on the negative stuff.

4. Different personalities could still be a perfect match:

If you're thinking, "Hey, I'm an engineer, and my date is a lawyer, I don't think we will click well," well then, you're clearly mistaken. You don't have to date someone of the same field as yours. You may fear that they might have a different approach than you on several things, and you might even disagree with them on some of the stuff, but this is precisely what makes this experience beautiful. You got to step out of your comfort zone, explore your options, and know that the other person can be just as interesting as you wish them to be. Don't expect too much from them; after all, it's only a first date, and you don't want to disappoint either them or yourself. Robert Levenson says, "Different personalities may provide couples with complementary resources for dealing with life's challenges."

5. Look presentable, be presentable:

If you want to make a solid first impression and want the person to call you for a second date, you should focus on making yourself look flawless. From choosing the best outfit that would go with the weather to wearing your favorite scent and making a neat hairstyle, you have to up your game. This will not only impress your date but would also bring you a sense of self-confidence. Hygiene is one of the major things people notice in others, especially when meeting for the first time. Be aware of your body language. No matter how nervous you are, you have to be calm and relaxed in Infront of your date. Try mirroring the movements of your date to show them that you're interested in what they have to say. The study says that the more we are attracted to someone, the more we mimic them. So, make sure you give your date positive signs.

6. Give them the fitting follow-up:

Say your date has been successful. The question arises, what next? Asking them out on another date right then and there might put them in an awkward position, as they didn't have enough time to ponder on this one yet. It could also make you feel like you're rushing things. On the other hand, you might be eager to hang out with them soon because you have felt that connection, the conversation with them flowed smoothly, and you have a ton of things in common. The best you can do is say that you had a great time with them and wish to meet them soon. You can text them after a few days for another date. But try not to sound too desperate and don't expect a reply right away. Maybe, you'll get a text from them to meet even before you're ready for another date. Just hope for the best and be patient.

Conclusion:

Success in life doesn't get handed to you on a silver plate, even if it's related to dating. You have to work hard in this area of your life too. If your date doesn't go as you have planned it to, have no worries, there's plenty of fish in the sea. You could learn from your mistakes and avoid them on your following dates, till you get a perfect one. Learn from the experiences. And if you do get a perfect date, then way to go!

PART 2

Chapter 1:
6 Ways To Deal With Manipulative Partners

<u>Intro:</u>

Manipulative partners are those that disguise your interests as their interests. These people will manipulate you and make you feel like what they think are facts. They will make you feel like you are incompetent, arrogant, and crazy then offer help to improve your life and attitude. In a relationship, it is natural and easy to be influenced by your partner; this can also change the way you make decisions. Such partners make you believe that you should do exactly what they tell you, or your life will be ruined. But actually, they do not want to help you; they are just controlling you. If you got worried listening to all this and then keep watching until the end, we will tell you eight ways to identify and deal with manipulative partners!

1. **Understanding Manipulation in a Relationship**

Firstly, to get things done in their own way, they will make you feel guilty and appeal to your insecurities. If you have seen these two things in your partner, then they are manipulating you. Now, this manipulativeness can manifest itself in multiple ways. It can include unfair teasing, passive-aggressiveness, and sarcasm now. Manipulation is not always easy to pinpoint because every case is different from the other. If you can very easily identify it, then it might not be manipulation. The one way you can figure out you are being manipulated is if you are doing things that are different than your gut reaction and the decisions you are taking are to satisfy others. Well, suppose this sounds similar to you. In that case, you need to take a step back from the particular situation and reflect on whether you are being manipulated signs are you have been ignoring the red flags. Still, if you take time out, you will see whether your partner is trying to control you or not.

2. Be Objective:

You need to look at your partner's behavior with practical eyes in order to figure out whether they are manipulative or not. The most challenging part could be acknowledging that the manipulation is happening in the first place because this will require self-awareness, courage, objectivity, and being conscious of patterns of behavior. You will need to be extremely honest with yourself when considering your partner's behavior. Do not justify their behavior, do not look at the situation with rose-colored glasses. Think what you would say if a friend explained the same situation to you; what advice would you give them. Whatever you think for your friend, you should apply the same thing to yourself.

3. Approach your Partner with a Plan:

Now you know your situation best, only you know the level of manipulativeness and whether you want to resolve the issue or just leave. But first, you will have to find out whether you can resolve the issue or not to bring up your feelings to your partner. But before you do that, spend a good amount of time thinking about the best possible way you could do it because your partner can respond in any way. It could be something you did not even predict they can act hurt or offended, and that will further appeal to your insecurities. Now, when you confront a manipulator, there is a high risk of being further manipulated now; this situation is completely dependent on how skilled they are and how self-aware you are. Remember to always maintain an objective attitude and not blame your partner. When you are talking to your partner, always use 'I' statements and itemize how you are being manipulated. If you use clear language, there are high chances that your partner will reply positively, and this will turn into a constructive conversation.

4. Be Open to Your Partner's Opinion:

You will get an idea of whether or not the problem will be solved by how your partner will handle your feelings. You should allow them to explain themselves; there are chances that they are not doing this consciously. Although manipulation has a negative connotation to it, it is not always the source of evil. If the manipulator owns his behavior, then you will be able to have healthy, effective communication. But in case your partner gets angry or becomes defensive, you will have to think about your next move carefully. When you figure out, you are being manipulated, and the next move will vary from person to person. Firstly, you need to decide whether you want to make it work with this person or not; whatever decision you make, you need to be self-aware.

We are going to list some measures you can adopt to avoid manipulative behavior.

5. Trust Your Judgment

You always need to trust your judgment, and you are the only one who knows what is best for your life. You might go around asking people about what you should do with your life, especially your partner and the people who are close to you. It is okay to be indecisive, but if you are looking for people to define you, you will come out as vulnerable, and you will be easier to manipulate. What will separate you from others is the ability to listen to your own beliefs. This will also set boundaries for you. When you hold onto your beliefs, it is harder for someone to manipulate you.

6. Stop Compromising:

Although guilt is a useless emotion, it can be used as a powerful tool. One weapon that will make it easy to manipulate you is guilt! Your partner can make you feel guilty about small mistakes, your past failures, and even for being confident and happy. They will make you feel that a person should not feel too good about themselves. Another weapon they use is doubt, and once they are able to instill self-doubt in you, you will doubt your worth and abilities. This state of uncertainty gives them more power.

Conclusion:

The best way to deal with a manipulative partner is to be very confident in yourself, and once you have figured out manipulative tendencies, talk to them about those. Communication is always the best solution.

Chapter 2:
7 Ways to Deal With Sexual Problems In A Relationship

Whether the problem is big or small, there are as many things as you can do to get your sex life back on track. Your sexual well-being goes hand in hand with your overall emotional, physical, and mental health. Sexual dysfunction is defined as the difficulty or issue that might arise for an individual as well as for the couple during any stage of intimacy. It is an overly stigmatized situation that is far more common than many people realize. Overcoming sexual dysfunction doesn't have to be as daunting as it may feel. There are many ways to handle the frustration without putting too much strain on your partner or the relationship.

Communicating with your partner, availing yourself of some of the many excellent self-help materials on the market, maintaining a healthy lifestyle, and just having it easy and fun can help you weather tough times. Here are some ways to deal with the sexual problems in your relationship.

1. **Know The Importance of Intimacy**

It is essential to notice when the intimacy starts to wane within their relationship. Couples need to understand that they won't have the same level of sexual drive or desires throughout their relationship. Intimacy is a significant element to help couples bond. We feel calm and connected when we experience love and physical contact. If you have started to feel like you and your partner are experiencing intimacy issues, address them and don't hide them out of sheer embarrassment and shame.

2. Remember That You Are Not Alone

Sexual dysfunction in all its forms is something that plagues countless couples. There's no need to feel isolated. There are always ups and downs in every couple's sex life, and the real problem arises when they don't know how to talk about sex or the issues related to it. The societal stigma surrounding sexual dysfunction and lack of communication skills and education serve as the basis for why the couples feel ashamed and isolated in addressing their issues.

3. Get Educated

Couples mainly set up unrealistic expectations about sex that lead them to nothing but disappointment. Couples need to realize that their sexual desires, preferences, and abilities will begin to change as they age. A couple should get themselves informed about sexuality, sexual intercourse, and sexual dysfunction to be well aware of the challenges that they are facing or might face ahead. An excellent way to get educated is by contacting a sex therapist or reading books if you are too shy to talk openly about it.

4. Don't Play The Blame Game

Suppose the challenges you're facing affect one partner only. In that case, it is significant to face the issue as a team and work through it together. It is critical to look at sexual dysfunction as a couple experiencing a problem, and not just one partner. There is nothing worse than blaming and isolating your partner. Without the said support and communication, the problem is more likely to be increased than to dissolve.

5. Communicate With Care

Don't attempt to discuss your sexual problems with your partner if they are already stressed out about something else. Remember, timing is everything. Carefully address the problem with your partner and choose soft words to convey your message. Before engaging in the discussion, make sure both of you are level-headed, calm, well-rested, and prepared to have the conversation. It could get quite emotional, so you both have to be careful.

6. Give Yourself Time

As you age, your sexual responses slow down, and it may need more time for you to get aroused. The physical changes in your body might now give a completely different perspective of your sexual desires and arousals. Working on these physical necessities into your lovemaking routine can open doors to a new kind of sexual experience for you.

7. Do Kegel Exercises

Improving sexual fitness is essential for both men and women. They can do so by exercising their pelvic floor muscles. To engage in these exercises, tighten the muscle you would use to stop the urine in midstream. Hold the contraction for 2-3 seconds and then release. Repeat this ten times, doing a set of five each day. These exercises can be done anywhere, whether driving, standing in a checking line, or sitting at home.

Conclusion

Sexual dysfunction might be one of the hardest things to overcome in a relationship and is undoubtedly one of the most challenging issues to communicate with your partner about. However, with a bit of hard work, and a lot of support and love from your significant other, there is always a hope that you and your partner will find a solution that will eventually bring back happiness into your lives.

Chapter 3:
7 Signs You Are Falling Out of Love

Love is the most beautiful, magical, and natural feeling that one can experience. Falling in love releases the chemicals that might make you feel like you're on top of the world. It even mimics the high sensation one feels while on cocaine. But nothing gold can stay. It means that nothing lasts forever, so enjoy and cherish it while you can. Falling out of love is just as natural as falling into it; it's neither of the individual's fault, and no one should be blamed.

According to the American Psychological Association, more than 40% of all marriages in the United States end in divorce, and in general, the rate of breakups of romantic relationships is much higher. Every relationship goes through its ups and downs. According to Jane Greer, Ph.D., a family and marriage therapist based in New York City, "Being able to sort out the ambivalence is at the heart of every relationship."

Instead, a single event doesn't cause the breakup of a committed relationship; it slowly builds over time and then comes crashing down in an instant. Here are some signs that may show that either you or your partner is falling out of love.

1. You Feel Annoyed At Everything They Do.

The sound of their voice that you once found charming, the haircut that you always liked on them, or even if they're breathing in your direction, if you find yourself simply annoyed by all of it, there is a bigger issue there. The snoring or the way they eat, or any other mannerisms that you avoided before, now becomes evident and irritating to you, this is not a good sign for your relationship. Their little quirks and imperfections that you once found adorable are now starting to get on your nerves. You feel resented towards them. This tendency to overlook your partner's positive attributes and completely shift your focus to the negative ones could signal that you are falling out love very quickly.

2. You Feel Happier Around Others Than With Your Partner

Your face lights up whenever you see a friend, or you put up a good face when you enter the room full of your family or co-workers but you act all dim and glum when you're around your partner without knowing why you're being that way. What's happening is that you're now getting the emotional connection and fulfilment from others that you were once receiving from your partner. You put more effort and energy into engaging in conversations with others than with your partner. This gravitation towards spending time with your friends rather than your partner shows that you just genuinely feel more relaxed and happier around them, which is not a good sign for the relationship.

3. Your Priorities Have Changed

Remember how you used to hover and cling around your partner when you both first started dating? You couldn't get tired from listening to all about their day and telling them about yours. But now, you've put everything and everyone else first but your partner. You would rather talk to a friend or see a movie with a colleague, rather than spending time with your partner. You purposely avoid them, don't reply to their texts, or answer their calls immediately. You make them wait for when it's convenient for you to call them back. This disinterest in your partner is a sure-fire sign that you are slowly falling out of love.

4. You Don't Want To Talk About It

You seem to be more distant than usual, and your partner noticed it. You refused to talk about it and avoided the confrontation, and let them think whatever they're thinking. You start to keep things to yourself and do not tell them if something's wrong or bothers you. They remain silent during arguments or just agree with you to end the discussion. This is what people do when they no longer want to fight for the relationship. They start to distance themselves slowly and gradually from their partner. If you catch yourself feeling like you don't want to deal with any problems you may have with your partner, you may be down that path as well.

5. You Don't Feel Excited to Spend Time with Them

The two of you were inseparable in the beginning. You used to count the minutes till you can finally see and meet them again. And now, it has started to feel like a burden or a duty. You don't get excited anymore to be with them. You feel yourself being reserved and quiet around them, not having the energy to talk or communicate. You just act like a robot, sitting there with a plain face and no emotions whatsoever, nodding at everything your partner says and not engaging in conversations with him. You now look at the clock continuously and hope that the time passes by quickly so you can get into your personal space again, away from your partner. When the spark and joy of hanging out with your partner fades, it is tough for you to connect with them on a deeper emotional level. You may simply be dragging your feet along this relationship.

You Have Stopped Thinking About A Future Together

The most important aspect of a relationship is when you can picture yourself and your partner being together in the future. You can't wait to spend the rest of your lives together and can't stop thinking about the adventures that the coming years of life will bring you. But if you have stopped envisioning your partner in that future you want to have, then he's not the one for you. Your future with them starts to feel blurry, and you're anxious and worried about them being in it. If you and your partner aren't on the same page in terms of future goals, then the sooner you both say goodbye to each other, the better.

You've lost respect for them.

Respect is more crucial than love when it comes to relationships. Respect is gained through trust and support and the fact that your partner would always be there for you whenever needed. If the mutual respect is gone, then your relationship is pretty much done for. You might have even sacrificed your self-respect to save your relationship many times, but all in vain. It's time to put your chin up and move on because the relationship might not be fixable.

Conclusion:

Take some alone time and think about all the aspects that make you fall out of love with your partner. If you want to save your relationship at any cost, take a break from your partner and see if your feelings change. Or simply talk it through with him, the things that are bothering you, and the stuff he does that make you feel bad. In the end, it takes a lot of effort to keep up the spark alive. But if yours is burned out, there's nothing you can do rather than move on from it.

Chapter 4:
7 Signs You Cannot Handle A Relationship

You have always romanticized the idea of perfect love. As a result, you're always looking out for that special someone who will sweep you off of your feet. And luckily, after working your fingers to the bone (as well as some bits of stalking, well, GUILTY!), you have found the person that you will now proudly call "the one."

But before you know it, you're now facing challenges and struggling to keep your relationship working. It was all candlelight dinners and slow dances a month ago, but now the issues seem more like giant summits than small stumbling blocks. The relationship is turning sour all of a sudden, and you can't help but notice the things that are making it like that.

You might start acting weird with your partners due to constant overthinking of "what if." What if the person will break my heart in the future? What if my partner is hiding some dark secret? What if we won't work out? What if they will hurt me so much that I won't be able to recover or move on? All of these worst-case scenarios will tend to put you in a state of anxiety, and it will affect your relationship with your partner just as well.

Here are 7 signs that will help you identify why your relationship is falling off the bridge.

1. Self-absorbed behavior:

Perhaps the primary aspect of working a relationship is by taking care of your partner's wants and needs. You have to make them feel special now and then by either making small sacrifices or large, meaningful gestures. Taking care of yourself and prioritizing your own needs are important. Still, if you tend to ignore what your partner wants, ultimately, it may cause some problems. Being utterly selfish and not addressing your partner's needs will make them feel cut out from your life. Always praising yourself and not appreciating the things that your partner does for you is a complete setback. This will lead to frustration and confrontation, and your partner might end up arguing and fighting you about it.

2. You run away from the word "commitment":

Spending a huge chunk of your time with your partner, going on trips with them, loving them, and clinging to them all seem just fine to you. But as soon as they talk about the future or getting married, you either get awkward, freak out, or avoid discussing it overall. You make your partner feel unsure about where the two of you are heading with this relationship. You're always talking about your relationship in the present tense and withdraw immediately if the word "commitment" or "future" comes up.

3. Lack of communication:

Communicating effectively is perhaps the most vital element in any relationship. Suppose you don't open up to your partner emotionally. In that case, that means you don't want to invest yourself in the relationship entirely. We all are busy in this fast-pacing world, but if we don't give our bare minimum time to our partners, tell them how we feel, or ask them about their emotional needs, we will drift physically and emotionally further from them. We might also end up acting in a passive-aggressive manner, which could in turn affect our relationship negatively. Your partner might end up having self-doubts about themselves, thinking they are not worthy enough to know the critical aspects of your life, and feeling that they are not a priority to you. This would lead to both of you being more and more distant from each other.

4. **Over Dependency:**

Linking our moods with our partners, making them feel responsible about everything that's happening in our lives, is the biggest red flag that indicates we cannot handle our relationship well. Our happiness should not always depend on others, and instead, we should try to be satisfied in our alone environment. We should give ourselves and our partners a safe space, spend time with ourselves, pamper and care for ourselves; not try to get on the nerves of our partners. To quote RuPaul, "If you can't love yourself, how in the hell are you gonna love somebody else?" Being vulnerable with someone is a healthy aspect of one's relationship, but being excessively clingy and needy can be a considerable drawback.

Showing these sides too much can wreck the harmony and balanced dynamic between you and your partner. If you have low self-esteem, you might look at your relationship in black and white terms; I.e., as either all good or all bad. This will lead to some severe issues in communication and perception.

5. Getting insensibly jealous:

Being jealous is a part of human nature. We can't deny the feelings of jealousy and possessiveness for our loved ones, even if we try so hard to. But the key is to manage that jealousy so that it wouldn't become a drain in your relationship. We all have our pasts and exes, and if you feel like you can't hear about any of your partner's exes or crushes, you cannot handle the relationship well. Jealousy usually comes from some deep long-forgotten insecurities. So, if you feel like you're getting irritated and jealous over petty things, or you might have become controlling towards your significant other, then your relationship may be in danger.

6. You're not patient:

When it comes to working a relationship out, you might not want to lose your cool now and then. Sure, your partner would test your limits; they would have a deficient phase or might take out all their frustration and anger on you. But suppose you retaliate with the same things instead of consoling and comforting your partner. In that case, you can't handle your relationship. If you're impatient with your partner, get annoyed or irritated with their little things, or always tries to find something to fight about, you might want to reconsider the relationship as a whole.

7. **Inconsistency:**

Inconsistency is perhaps the most major turn-off in any relationship. No one wants themselves to be hanging by a thread. Suppose you make your partner feels unsure about your feelings for them or give them mixed signals. In that case, the relationship might soon slip away from your hands. One day you're making them feel like they're on top of the world, and the next, you're crashing them down on the ground. You are not willing to make efforts for them and just going with the flow. You're avoiding their confrontations and not listening to their cries of help about letting them be clear about what you feel about them. This might frustrate your partner to the point that they might be willing to cut all the ties off.

Conclusion:

Being in a relationship isn't easy. It's all blood, sweat, and tears. But the more you make efforts for the people you love, the easier it will get for you. If you relate to the signs above as to why you can't handle a relationship well, try working on them and yourself to better your relationship. On the other hand, if you're unwilling to make any efforts, do your partner a favor, have a serious talk with them, and with all your heart and soul, let them go! Don't keep them selfishly under your wings if you are not ready to commit or compromise in the relationship. The best decision is to go your separate ways and find your true source of happiness elsewhere.

Chapter 5:
7 Signs That You Were Never In Love

It may seem like a bed of roses and candles in the initial days of your relationship. Everything seems brighter and phenomenal. You may think you've found the perfect partner for yourself. You may even convince yourself that you're in love with this person. When, in reality, you're stuck in a dysfunctional fantasy-based relationship that's draining the life out of you.

One minute you're drooling over them, and the next minute you're left wondering if it was really loved or not. Sometimes, we get this euphoric feeling with someone and mistakes it for love. Once the relationship ends, you start to figure out if what you had with your partner was real or if it was just a façade. Love requires efforts, showing vulnerability, caring for the other person, and having the guts to leave when needed.

Here are 7 signs to show you that you never really were in love (even though you might think you were).

1. The Relationship Moved Too Fast

If you haven't really known each other for a long time but said the three magical words right away, then my dear, it's not love but infatuation. As Elizabeth Gilbert once said, "being in love is not the same as love; it's more like the dodgy second cousin of love who always borrows money and can't keep a job." Infatuation produces a flood of dopamine and norepinephrine, which stimulates feelings of cravings, loss of appetite, sleeplessness, intense energy, and focused attention, which may leave you confusing it for love. A relationship can't survive off the great chemistry alone. You need to know the other person, understand them, see their flaws and faults, and accept them for who they are. True love thrives and blooms over time, and doesn't just happens in an instant.

2. You're Better Off Without Them

When you genuinely love someone, you tend to always think about them and care for them. On the other hand, if you rarely care for your partner, your mind doesn't drift off to them, and you no longer think about their needs, their happiness, or their whereabouts. Stephen J. Betchen, the author of 'Magnetic Partners,' says, "Partners who are in love tend to maintain a focus on their counterparts." This means that if your mind drifts off from the idea of them, your heart will soon follow. Over time, you stop caring altogether for your partner and the relationship has effectively ended. Maybe in that situation you never loved your partner in the first place to maintain a focus on them enough.

3. You Never Open Up To Each Other Emotionally

Love is much more than the physical attraction and the honeymoon phase. It's about being vulnerable to your partner and showing them what you're really like from the inside. It's about being honest in sharing your feelings and emotions, no matter how bad it will affect your relationship, and then figuring it out together. If your partner didn't give you the reassurance that you needed to open up or if they didn't care enough to talk about your own feelings, then you may not have been in love with them.

4. You Feel Like You're Not Good Enough For Them

Relationship expert and psychotherapist Emily Mendez, M.S. EdS, says that if you don't feel like you deserve them, then that could mean you're not meant to be. When you're with the right person, you have this urge always to be yourself, no matter how goofy or messy you look. You feel completely comfortable around them and trusts that they find you amazing regardless. But if you feel like you need to change yourself or feel like your true self isn't good enough, then that's a clear sign that you both are not meant to be together. The next time you catch yourself having to put up a façade around your partner, ask yourself if you really love the person or if the person really loves you back for who you are.

5. You Spend Most of Your Time Being Stressed Out in The Relationship

While there were some fantastic moments in your relationship, the bad ones weighed them down overall. The baseless arguments, yelling, screaming, exchanging hurtful words, and disrespect became the forte of your relationship. There was far more stress and conflict than it should've been. Every day it's a new and senseless topic that you both find yourself arguing about. True love is all about sorting things out and minimizing conflicts. It's about producing positive emotions and respectfully listening to your partner's point of view, even if you disagree with them.

If frequent conflicts is the hallmark of your relationship, it may be time to call it quits.

6. You Don't Seem to Bother To Connect With Their Family or Friends

If you really love someone, the first thing that you think is to establish a future and settle down with them. You really look forward to connecting with your partner's family and friends and get to know more about him from them. You're also nervous at the back of your mind and secretly crossing your fingers, hoping that they might like you. You're willing to be approved and accepted by them. But, if you're least bothered about meeting his family or friends, or just casually meets them with a cold face, then you never really were in love in the first place. The lack of desire and interest says a lot about how you view the relationship.

7. There's Something Off About the Relationship

One day you're at each other's necks, breaking things off. And the next day, you're back together again. According to Jenna Matlin, Clairvoyant Intuitive of The Queen of Wands Tarot says, "I have done probably about 5000 readings in the last six years as a full-time intuitive, and from that, I can tell you I have never seen an on-again, off-again relationship work out." It would be best to cut ties with unhealthy and toxic situations to make way for healthy and happy relationships to come your way. You might have put in a lot of your time, energy, and effort to make this relationship work, but if your gut is telling you to move on, please do that.

Conclusion:

We can never be sure if someone is "The One" for us. Letting go of a relationship is never easy, primarily when you have invested so much of your time and emotions in that. But time is undoubtedly the best healer. You and your partner both need someone they can share their true love with. Holding onto something that you know is eventually going to fail is pitiable. Find yourself someone you can be pure and effortless with.

Chapter 6:
7 Ways To Be More Mature In A Relationship

Intro:

Even if we love someone with all our heart, the reality of this life will be a reminder for us that nothing is ever as simple as it seems. You can ask anyone who has ever been in a relationship, and they will tell you that love is just one of the component you need for a committed relationship. But the important thing they will you that is essential for a relationship is maturity. Maturity is a skill that is not acquired from instinct and is instead learned. So, you might be wondering how one can act maturely in a relationship? Well, listen on, and you will get your answers.

1. **Learn the values of respect, trust, and sincerity:**

These are the essential ingredients of a healthy and happy relationship, and you should learn them as soon as you can. First, you need to trust your partner that they have the strength to fight for what you have. Second, you should appreciate their sincerity and also express genuine affection and love towards each other. Lastly, you should respect them as human being and as a person.

2. **Address the needs of the relationship first:**

When you are in a committed relationship, you are not thinking and making decisions for yourself and the other person, so there is no room for selfishness. Being mature in a relationship means working on your goals and making the right decisions that are beneficial for yourself and your partner. Whatever plans you have, they should be focused on the needs and wants of both of you because the consequences will affect not only your future but also theirs.

3. Accept the reality that people are not perfect:

When you get through your partner's bad moods and terrible tantrums and accept the worst parts of them, there is a huge chance that you guys are going to end up together. You have to accept the fact that the person you are in love with is not perfect; everyone has their flaws, and that is the beauty and complexity of a human, and once you accept that and see the beauty in them despite their flaws, that means you really love them, and that is also the mature move. However, you should always be aware that if they stoop too low, you should help them grow.

4. Practice patience and choose forgiveness:

The person you love can make you the happiest and at the same time break your heart in a million pieces. Love makes us vulnerable, and hence we get hurt easily. But you have to realize that just like you, your partner is only a human, and they can also make mistakes without realizing it. There can be moments when you will feel you are being taken for granted or that you have been betrayed, but you should not let these moments get to you. You should have patience, and that patience will give you strength, and when you forgive them, it will give you hope that everything is part of the process.

5. Relationships can't be perfect:

As we just mentioned, there will be days when the love of your life will break your heart or make you feel bad. And there are also going to be times when your wrong choices will affect your relationship or hurt your significant other. So, in those times, you should not lose hope and realize that no relationship is perfect and everything you are going through is just part of the process, and all the challenges you face will either make you or break you. But, you should be mature enough to not let them break you.

6. Recognize the power of words:

Words are extremely powerful; once you have said something, you can not take it back. Your words can make someone's day and can also make someone feel horrible about themselves. Therefore, you should make an active effort to learn what you should not express and what to say. Of course, you have the right to express whatever you are feeling, and it can be both good and bad, but you should never use this freedom to hurt the person you love the most.

7. Destructive consequences of overthinking:

One of the signs of maturity is to not let your destructive and damaging thoughts consume you. These destructive thoughts can ruin your relationship and even end it. Many younger couples do not have faith in their partners, which is the reason for their breakups, so it is important for mature adults to not act in the same way and let go of small things because, in the bigger picture, they will not matter.

Conclusion:

Life is difficult, and it takes a lot of time and maturity to figure it out and being in a relationship can make things complicated. So, even if you have lost someone because you were still figuring out things, you do not have to lose heart because you will soon find someone better.

Chapter 7:
7 Ways to Keep Your Relationship Fresh

Anyone who's in a relationship wants to know the secret to make their love life last. And while everyone's relationship is different, the couples should thrive to keep the spark alive for years or even decades. Being in love is beautiful on the one hand but complex on the other. It takes a lot of time, sacrifices, effort, and adjustments to nurture a relationship that will leave you happy and satisfied. However, over some time, partners tend to get bored with each other and end up finding ways to keep the relationship excited.

No matter what type of a relationship you are in, be it a marriage, casual dating, or exploring open relationships, the bonds form with another gets more substantial and more meaningful when you explore new things together, have love and respect for each other, and be grateful for each other every day. From the mundane to the extra special, there are many things to keep a relationship fresh and exciting.

Here are 7 ways to keep your relationship fresh.

1. **Be Adventurous**

It's essential to take risks with your partner to keep things interesting. The key is to be adventurous together and push one another to try new things. Sure, it might sound scary at first, but you will always have your partner to support and push you. If it's something that you have a phobia of, but your partner loves it, try it for their sakes.

2. Show Gratitude

Gratitude goes a long way in any relationship. Simply saying thank you to your partner more often and with a kind the intention will make both you and your partner feel good and closer to each other. Several studies suggest that showing gratitude goes along with lower levels of depression, anxiety, and envy. Appreciate them for their ideas, views, opinions, and the things they do for you, no matter how small or big they may be. Do something special for them to tell them how much they mean to you.

3. Treat As You Want To Be Treated

Give your partner the same things that you wish to receive from them. Whether it's your love, passion, generosity, and kindness, or your quirks, phobias, traumas, and insecurities, loving someone comes with all sorts of nuances. Make sure to ask your partner what they need, and don't hesitate to communicate with your partner clearly and tell them what you want. It would be best if you first were the way you want your partner to be. Treat each other with kindness, respect, and compassion.

4. Take A Considerable Risk Together

It may sound a little crazy, but this is exactly what couples need. Switching up your life in a big way can help strengthen your bond with your partner in unimaginable ways. One of the best ways to create a closer connection is to do something risky, like move to a new city, or a state, or even a country. It may sound dramatic, but it all comes down to choosing to face risks together. Whenever life throws at us a difficult choice, we pick the scariest thing and grow through it.

5. Have Date Nights

Between your busy life and all the extracurricular stuff, you might think that a date night would sound unnecessary or extravagant. But scheduling a date night would just be what you and your partner need! Date nights are the dedicated times for you and your partner to connect and have fun together. It's an escape from whatever good or bad is going on in your life right now. You can worry about the bills and the to-do lists later. For now, make it all seem to go away and enjoy the time that you two have in hand.

6. Spend Time Alone

Yes, you heard that right. Spend some time alone, without your partner. While we are all about fun date nights and moving to another city, spending time with yourself is equally important. When we have some alone time, we self-analyze and self-reflect and bring all this knowledge of self-awareness to our partner. It helps you connect with yourself on a deeper level and gives you the benefit of looking at yourself and ask, "Am I someone I'd want to be with?"

7. Do The Things They Like (Even If You Don't Like Them Much)

You should accompany your partner from time to time to the things they enjoy doing, even if it's not really your thing. Be it shopping, golfing, swimming, or any other activity, you should take part in it unless there's a specific reason or you not to. Be generous, open-minded, and graceful in what your partner is interested in. Even if it bores you to death, your partner will feel appreciated and happy, and this will bring both of you closer to each other.

Conclusion

Choose to love your partner no matter what. Know that we all are full of flaws, but our true strength lies in accepting the quirks and shortcomings of the people we love. Help them get into a good mood; surprising and appreciating them are vital elements to a lasting relationship. You don't have to go overboard, and just a few small meaningful gestures will suffice.

Queen Of Hearts

PART 3

Chapter 1:
7 Signs you're More Attractive Than You Think

We feel conscious about ourselves every now and then. We are our own biggest critics. Finding flaws in ourselves sometimes leads to constructive criticism, which in turn leads to self-development. But sometimes, the constructive criticism might lead to a self-destructive reproach that will disturb the healthy and happy life you're living. It's normal to have self-doubts, wondering how people see us or what they think about us.

We live in a society where there is constant pressure to look your best self. People might point out our flaws and weaknesses, but what matters is how we emerge from it all. A study by Feynman in 2007 revealed that the way people see us determines how they will treat us. So, it's best if we remain confident and comfortable in our skin. Our appearances can either make or break the first impression of how people will perceive us. Research in 2016 by Lammers, Davis, Davidson, and Hogue revealed that first impressions could have a lasting effect on our relationship with the other person.

Many of us are used to being hard on ourselves. So it practically seems like a joke that anyone would find us attractive. Here are 7 signs that will confirm that you're more attractive than you think!

1. You rarely get compliments:

I know many of you wouldn't believe this but just hear me out first. Have you ever put on your most fabulous outfit, put on that sexy cologne, and dressed up all stunning from head to toe? You were confident enough that all eyes would be on you, and you will receive tons of compliments. But by the end of it all, you have hardly received any! Naturally, this would lead to you having some severe self-doubts about yourself. But you needn't worry. Psychology says that whenever we see a gorgeous person, we assume that he/she might have very high self-esteem. As a result, people rarely compliment those people. People also think that you already know how stunning you look, and you might be getting a lot of attention already. So, they avoid complimenting you too much. Instead of treating the scarcity of compliments as a bad thing, just maybe you are already the subject of many secret admirers.

2. The Compliments you get feel insincere:

Finally, you're receiving those compliments that you have been waiting for, for so long. But to your surprise, they sound apathetic and emotionless. You're confirmed now that you don't come off quite as attractive to other people. But we have a theory on this too. Suppose there is a gorgeous friend of yours. Do you constantly flatter them and gush about their appearance? You don't. You only compliment them if they're wearing a new outfit or changed their looks. The same happens to you. People think you already know how beautiful you are, so they don't pay much attention to the compliments they give you. The sole reason why the compliments sound so mundane and trivial. So, if you have been experiencing this, then you're more attractive than you think.

3. **People get nervous around you:**

Whenever you enter a room, you notice people suddenly being all nervous around you. This may happen because they're caught off guard by how gorgeous you look. They may feel pressured to make an excellent first impression since you've already made a perfect one on them. As a result, they try to hide their flaws in In front of you. They might become either too confident or underconfident. People tend to become awkward and nervous when they see other people as too attractive or too perfect.

4. **You find yourself locking eyes with a lot of people:**

We, humans, tend to stare at the desirable things we want. Research by the University of Oslo in 2015 found that your brain gives you a dopamine shot when you look at something pleasurable. While it may not always be the case that people staring at you might find you attractive. Sometimes it can just be a mistake, or maybe you have worn your shirt wrong, or there's something stuck on your teeth, but a lot of times, we stare and lock eyes with the people we find good-looking. So, if a person keeps staring at you even if you have caught them and passes a smile, it definitely means he likes what he's staring at.

5. **People are surprised by your insecurities:**

People might become shocked when you tell them about your complexes and insecurities. They think that since you're so gorgeous, you have nothing to worry about. But we all have our bad days where we go through self-doubts and low self-esteem. People wouldn't see this as such a problem because they would love to look like you and don't even notice the flaws you point out about yourself. Instead, they might become irritated when you complain about your issues because you look so self-confident and self-sufficient to them.

6. **People are often too polite or too unfriendly to you:**

You find people being either too optimistic or too pessimistic around you. They either might be too warm and friendly or too harsh and rude when you first meet them. The truth is, people, tend to react strongly to the people they find attractive. Some people might find excuses to spend time with you and praise you, while others may sound too petty around you. This might also be because of the jealousy they may feel towards you. A positive person will always see you as an equal and will always treat you with a polite and friendly attitude.

7. **People are interested in you:**

You might feel people asking a lot of questions about you and getting to know you better. They carry the conversation and like talking to you from time to time. Even though your communication skills are pretty average, they would still speak to you with the same interest. This is because they might think that you would have a great personality. After all, you have a pretty face. They would become compromising and would jump at the first opportunity to help you. We tend to be friendlier and more generous to the people subconsciously we find attractive. By helping you, they want to look good in your eyes too.

Conclusion:

You need to look past your insecurities, embrace your flaws, and accept the characteristics that people value in you. Don't forget that in the end, a good heart always wins over good looks. Don't become a victim of societal pressure and mould yourself into a perfect and flawless human being. There is nothing more attractive than appreciating yourself with all the good and the bad and knowing your worth. Find happiness in being vulnerable and weak, through the tough and challenging times. Life is a roller coaster ride, so you shouldn't have a need to feel perfect all the time!

Chapter 2:
7 Ways To Deal With Growing Apart In A Relationship

According to Ashley Davis Bush, LCSW, a psychotherapist who specializes in couple therapy, "It's incredibly easy for couples to grow apart because we have such busy lives." Change is inevitable. And while growing together is the vital key to last any relationship, we simply can't deny the fact that people evolve and change as time goes by.

If you go to sleep at night and wake up every morning knowing there's this one person in your life who loves you and has your back no matter what, then consider yourself very fortunate. But if you are in a relationship that has lost its passion or is struggling, you're probably suffering from the pain and frustration that's coming from the lack of love and support in your life. There could be a million reasons why your relationship isn't what it used to be. But the most common answer for the 80% of couples who get separated or divorced is, "we grew apart."

Here are 7 ways to deal with growing apart in a relationship.

1. **Talk About It**

Communication is the key to any healthy relationship. Let your partner know how you are feeling, and then get some ideas on how you both can get closer again. Being honest with your partner might work out brilliantly. You could start off by saying, "I really want to feel close to you again," or "it seems like we may be growing apart; how can we fix it?"

This will invite collaboration instead of the usual blame game. Maybe you will start to schedule more time together, get away for the weekend, or seek a couple of counseling. It's better to start off early than to wait till your whole relationship is damaged.

2. **Bring Back Old Habits or Try Some New Ones**

Sometimes you have to go down memory lane and recall the activities or things that brought both of you closer. Go into the flashbacks and see what helped you grow together? Maybe you both loved exercising together, or perhaps you both liked trying new restaurants. On the contrary, relationships thrive on novelty. You have to make sure that you're keeping things exciting and enjoyable by trying out new stuff.

3. **Ask Meaningful Questions**

Couples must remain interested in one another if they want to avoid growing apart. One of the many ways to do it is to deepen the conversation and allow access to the partner's inner thoughts and feelings. For example, if your partner is complaining about work, instead of suggesting solutions, ask them what would help them get through it and what they are feeling at that moment. You could ask about your partner's fears and doubts and appreciate them for everything they do for you.

4. Be Curious About Your Partner's Needs and Behaviors

It isn't easy to stay connected when one partner is a cat, and the other is a puppy. Meaning, one partner might need some space during the different needs closeness and reassurance. Over time, these slight differences could create conflict, frustration, and distance. But instead of giving into frustrations, trying being curious about what your partner wants. Try to get to the bottom of why your partner acts like that. Don't take their behaviors personally but instead assume the best and work towards making your partner and yourself feel relaxed and stress-free.

5. Fight Productively

Having good communication in your relationship also includes fighting productively. Couples shouldn't avoid conflict just because they don't want to get out of the honeymoon phase. By doing this, they suppress their feelings and emotions for fear of being different. Conflict is OK, but crossing the line while fighting or arguing isn't. Fighting the right way can help strengthen your bond, and it can also help you understand each other a lot more.

6. Be Kind To Each Other

One of the significant reasons to keep your relationship from growing apart is to be kind to each other. It's a simple thing, but many couples tend to overlook its importance with time. Being kind is as easy as complimenting your partner or doing something thoughtful for them. It's crucial to show kindness as much as you can. It can go a long way and helps make couples deposits in their love bank so that they can withdraw it and have fuel when the times are rough.

7. Practice Radical Acceptance

Practice the art of radical acceptance for having a long and happy partnership. This means that you should accept your partner as they are and resist the urge to fight the things that you can't change. Both partners should accept each other's imperfections, flaws, and quirks. Please stop trying to change their essential nature.

Conclusion

Maintaining a long-term relationship isn't easy. Many couples grow apart with time. But you have to understand that your relationship is like a gift in your life. You have to nurture it, be grateful for it, and do everything in your power to keep it thriving. If you're feeling distant in a relationship, the chances are that your partner is feeling the same. Be open with each other, and decide how you want to grow together.

Chapter 3:
7 Signs You've Outgrown Your Friendship

Growing up, we have always listened to the phrase "friendships last forever." And while some of them may do, some are just destined to end with time. It's difficult to say goodbye to someone with whom you spend a very long time and have a lot of history together. All those years of laughing hysterically on the inside jokes, making fun memories, and offering a shoulder to cry on whenever one of the two of you were struggling, putting an end to these might be more painful than you have thought so.

As children, we felt that our friends wouldn't ever change, and everything would remain just the same. But as it turns out, adulthood brings a significant amount of change into everyone's lives. As a result, our interests and priorities often diverge wildly when we enter our 20s and 30s, and by then, we start realizing that some of our friends might not be a good fit for us. And it's not because we have started to dislike them or did something unforgivable, instead because we have all simply changed.

Losing the thread of connection with a close friend can sometimes be more heart-breaking than ending a romantic relationship. But your well-being needs to acknowledge when a friendship has run its course. Here are a few signs that you've outgrown your friendship.

1. Your interactions feel draining:

If you get a sinking feeling in the pit of your stomach after you've made plans with them, rather than looking forward to it and thinking you would have a great time, then maybe it's time to reconsider the relationship with your friend. You may feel like whenever you two meet, the conversation focuses upon them, or they might bring up the topics you have little to no interest in. After hanging out with them, you feel emotionally drained, exhausted, and wrung out. You find them always complaining about their job or their relationship and asks you to listen to them and support them regardless. You're left feeling frustrated and angry and may vent to your other friends about this. These friendships tend to take more than they give and should eventually be ended.

2. You have nothing in common anymore:

Your conversations will be filled with awkwardness or constant arguments if you don't have anything in common with them. As communication is the key to maintain any relationship, having nothing to talk about would make you two feel bored, and the conversations would feel strained and unnatural. Maybe you two bonded over a shared interest that now seems childish and stupid. Eventually, your friendship would end because of the lack of substance in the relationship. People grow and people change, it could just be that you've outgrown your current friendship with the person.

3. You're the only one putting efforts:

You might feel that your friendship has become one-sided. You're the only one that's making sure to make plans and follow them up. You find yourself constantly checking up on them, being there for them in their good and their bad, congratulating them on their successes, and offering them their shoulder in crisis. But you see them constantly giving excuses not to make or cancel plans. You don't see them putting the same effort and consideration when it comes to you. It's like you are the only one who's working hard to make the friendship last. You're either requesting them or mocking them to put more effort, but the other person either will not or cannot comply. It is frustrating when the other party does not reciprocate. Maybe their lives have become so busy and you are no longer a priority to them. In that case, consider just letting this friendship drop by the wayside and move on to others who want to make time for you.

4. They're constantly judging and criticizing you:

In a healthy friendship, you wouldn't mind taking some honest criticism from your friends. After all, who knows us better than our friends? But if the complaint becomes constant and starts affecting your mental health, know that the friendship has become toxic. If your friend judges you on something that you've told them, or brings you down by making fun of you in front of everyone, or becomes jealous of your successes, then it's time for you to put an end to it. If you feel the negative energy whenever you're with them and ends up being more upset than happy, then it's a sign that maybe you've outgrown that friendship.

5. You've formed new friendships:

You've made new friends with whom you share similar goals, ask them for mature advice, or simply rely on them in your tough times. They support you throughout it all and help you deal with your career, family, and relationships. You find yourself wishing that your old friends could be more like them. But we can't change people. We have to accept that they are no longer the right fit for us, and maybe it's time for us to move on from the friendship.

6. You're in different phases of your life:

As the quote goes, "People come into your life for a reason, a season, or a lifetime." The most bittersweet end to a friendship would be if you're in different seasons of your lives and have started to drift apart slowly. Maybe you're going away for college, and they're still there living with their family. Or perhaps they are getting engaged, and you have just gone through a breakup. Maybe you have found a new job while they're still struggling to graduate. Perhaps you have found the meaning of your life in a different light while they're still stuck on the same page. Whatever it is, it's just an inevitable part of life that you might not be syncing up with the phase that they are in.

7. You've started to see them as immature and childish:

There was a time when their immature acts would look adorable to you. Now, they get on your nerves. They have started to cross all the boundaries, and when you confront them, they mask it with "I was just having fun with you." You two once shared the same sense of humor, but now your ideas and views have become different and aren't funny. They might joke about your insecurities, say hurtful and offensive things, and then becomes upset with you that you can't take a joke. Friends shouldn't drain your energy like this. They should support you and respect your boundaries and space, rather than violating them.

Conclusion:

No matter what stage or age you are in your life, remember that you are a free person. You shouldn't feel obliged to continue any relationship that threatens your mental peace and energy. Friends may fade, but the memories you made with them will live in your heart forever. Sure, it might be excruciatingly painful for the both of you to end the friendship, but you must do so maturely and on good terms. It's best to let the person go with whom you've outgrown your friendship and focus on the following aspects of your life.

Chapter 4:
6 Signs You Need To Give Yourself Some Personal Space

While we wish to stay forever in the honeymoon phase of a relationship, we also must keep in mind that it is precisely what we call it; only a phase. Not every relationship is sunshine and rainbows every day. A relationship is between two individuals who both have individual needs. Sometimes, those needs include having some alone time with themselves. But how and when exactly do you know if you need some space from your partner?

April Masini, a New York-based relationship expert and author, says, "If you can't make it an hour or two without checking in or asking a question of your partner, you need a break." Needing space in your relationship does not in any way means that you don't love your partner anymore; it simply means that you need some time to get recharge and take care of yourself. Here are some signs that you need to give yourself some personal space.

1. You Feel Stressed Out

Suppose you're unnecessarily stressed out, even if it isn't coming from your relationship. In that case, it's probably a good idea to spend some alone time and ponder over things. It can be some underlying tension coming from work or family, or it might be something in your relationship that you want but are not necessarily getting it. Taking some time out for yourself and figuring out where your stress is coming from or what's been upsetting you, you will then be better positioned to sort out your problems and discuss those issues with your partner.

2. You Don't Feel Like yourself

A significant sign indicating that you need some alone time for yourself is if you are started to feel exhausted, irritable, or simply just not yourself. Everyone should know the importance of needing some me time for yourselves. Your partner should understand if you need to take care of yourself and your mental health. Needing space from your partner in no way means that your relationship is at stake or if there's anything wrong with it. It simply means that you both need to spend time with yourself to rest, relax, or spend time with other people.

3. You Feel Suffocated

Spending so much time with people can prove fatal and can lead to being co-dependent on them, which is ultimately the kiss of death. It is assumed that, as a couple, you both should naturally be spending all of your time together, but there is such a thing as seeing too much of each other. It is essential to pull away and have some time for yourself. Find a hobby, take a walk, read a book. The more you spend your time with a person, the more likely you will get tired of each other soon. You need to get yourself some personal space not to get suffocated and overwhelmed by your relationships with other people.

4. You Don't Have any Outside Interests

Do you have any interests of your own, or do you rely entirely on the other person and their hobbies? It's healthy to have some things in common with your partner, but not all of them. Suppose you follow and copy their hobbies and interests and don't have any of your own. In that case, it might lead to some adverse psychological effects. Suppose they leave you or are just too busy to see you; you'll be left with nothing but boredom and waiting for the other person to catch up to you again. You need to give yourself space and find out what you like as an individual. Find your hobbies and passions, grow fond of them, and then work on them independently.

5. Spending Time With Them Is Draining You Out

If you aren't having as much fun as you used to have while meeting them, then you should take some space for yourself. If you're feeling drained out and low on energy after every interaction, it's time to spend some time apart. You get frustrated and irritated easily and don't make any efforts to resolve a fight. Patch-ups seem challenging for you; if your interactions are painful and difficult, then consider some alone time to gather your thoughts.

6. Your Vibe's Getting A Bit Off

Although there can be many reasons for this, stress, depression, exhaustion, etc., the primary cause can be that you're not getting enough space to deal with your emotions and feelings. Your relationship feels strained, and you feel like escaping from everything. This is the best time to ask for space from everyone and everything and ponder over whatever's bothering you.

Conclusion

Everyone deserves a relationship with more positivity than negativity in it. It's okay to need some space for yourself now and then. Evaluate your needs and try to figure out what you want.

Chapter 5:
7 Signs You're Becoming Toxic

Toxic is a word that's being thrown a lot about these days. Sure, we all struggle with our bad days. We sometimes tend to drift into our negative thoughts longer than expected. Still, suppose the situation is worsening instead of improving and is affecting those around us. In that case, we may have a condition called "toxicity."

But what exactly does it mean to be toxic? A toxic person is someone who harms others with their words or actions. They leave people exhausted, emotionally drained, negative, and worse off than before interacting with them. Sometimes the harm is felt instantly; other times, it slowly builds its way into people's lives. Sometimes the effect is short-term, while on other occasions, its influence seems long-term. A toxic person will tend to point out your flaws, even if things are going great your way. They would play the victim and would tend to bring you down with them.

A study published in the Journal of American Medical Association revealed that being in any kind of relationship with a negative person increases your risk of having heart disease, diabetes, and metabolism issues. This means that a toxic person not only affects our mental health but our physical health as well.

Here are 7 signs that will help you identify that you're becoming a toxic person:

1. You blame others for your problems:

Although it's one of the most challenging things to hold yourself accountable for what's going on in your life, it is perhaps the most vital one too. We are responsible for our words and actions, and we play a role (even if it's a minor one) in whatever problems arise in our lives. But blaming it on others constantly and playing the victim can make you a toxic person. Suppose, if a bad thing does happen in your life because of some other person, you should try to make efforts to be in a better position and find peace and happiness, rather than blaming them for your problems without having to address anything. A toxic person will always think that whatever tragedy he will surpass is because of the people around him. He will consider himself innocent and believe that the world is ready to come at him with knives.

2. You take more than you give:

Neediness is a part of human nature. There are some phases in our lives when we come off as needier than others. Sometimes we genuinely need help. And that's completely okay. There's nothing wrong with relying on the people you love for your support. But it gets tricky when the strings of your requests become never-ending. You always ask for their help but hides when in return, they ask for yours. You feel irritated if someone asks for your assistance and make excuses to avoid them. If you're doing this, it won't be long before people stop responding to your pleas. If you can't help them all in all, try just doing the bare minimum for them. Anything is better than nothing.

3. You're right, and they're wrong all the time:

There are loads of ways of being "right"; it's all about seeing other people's opinions, views, and perspectives. We might not always agree with them or have different ideas, but that does not mean we're always right and they're always wrong. There's a saying that asks an important question, "Do you want to be right, or do you want to be happy?" That said, it isn't realistic to achieve both of these at once. It would be best if you accepted that you can't always be correct. If you become irritated if your theory is proven wrong or someone doesn't agree with your facts, it might be hard to concede defeat to others. Still, it is essential for your mental peace.

4. You are critical of others:

You always tend to look at the negative aspects of others while ignoring their positive characteristics. Following the typical "crabs in a bucket mentality," you always tend to put others down. You like to harp on people's weaknesses and flaws to boost your self-esteem. You will verbally judge people's appearances, honest mistakes and speak poorly about them behind their backs. Even if they do something good, you tend to point out the flaws and make them feel bad about themselves.

This mentality is toxic and needs to be changed. We should always appreciate others no matter what.

5. You are inconsistent with your behavior:

Your behavior isn't stable if you're a toxic person. Your views, plans, and preferences could go one way today and another way tomorrow. You might become cold or cranky without any possible explanation. If someone asks you if anything's wrong, you tend to refuse it. But at the same time, you will let out a sigh or change your facial expression that will silently speak, "yes, there Is something wrong." But people aren't superhumans. You can't keep it in your heart and expect them to know what's bothering you magically. You're happy and content around people one day, and the next, they are dealing with your intense mood swings. Behaving this way will not only drain the people around you, but also cause many emotional and mental stresses for all parties involved. It is always better to be upfront with your thoughts and feelings.

6. You are manipulative and dishonest:

You feel the need to lie about everything, from things that are huge and important to the things that are tiny and meaningless. You make something up, exaggerates a matter, or twist and turn the facts for your convenience. You might manipulate or emotionally bully people around you to get them to do the things you want. You also might guilt trip them into getting things your way. You use their love, care, and support for your gains and do not even feel sorry about it. You think it's somehow their job to keep you satisfied and fulfilled by sacrificing their happiness. Catch yourself if the people around you start backing away from your life. You may not have realized that you have become that very person that you despise.

7. You disregard their boundaries:

A person always needs their safe space and boundaries. Suppose you have experienced people pushing you away and have requested you to stop acting a certain way. However, you still tend to violate their wishes. In that case, you unquestionably come under the category of toxic. Toxic people will also expect you to be available for them no matter what time of the day. It is almost impossible to keep a healthy and friendly relationship with someone who doesn't respect your boundaries. You might never know when they'll walk all over you.

Conclusion:

If you relate to the above signs above or knows someone around you who shows such symptoms, then you need to focus on yourself and search deep within you as to what is causing you to behave like this. A person can only put so much effort and give you a minimum amount of love and care, but changing yourself and being a better person for yourself and those around you is only in your hands. You have the power to change yourself from a toxic to a better person if you really try.

Chapter 6:
7 Signs That You're Ready To Take Your Relationship To The Next Level

If you're dating someone long enough, chances are you might know them well now and are ready to take your relationship to the next level. You both work out well together through all the ups and downs, connect with each other, and make each other's life wonderful. So whether you're thinking about making your relationship official by introducing them to your family and friends, moving in with them, or even getting engaged, it can both be scary and exciting when you think about making the relationship serious and taking that leap of faith.

While you should definitely consider if your partner is the perfect match for you, you should also do something that makes sure your partner doesn't slip off your hands. It's essential to keep your feelings honest to yourself and your partner because taking that next step would require being more open, vulnerable, and honest. If you feel that you have a healthy relationship, you can't imagine your life without your partner and are in a good place emotionally, then say no more. Here are some signs to convince you that you should up your game!

1. **You both trust each other fully:**

Being able to trust someone entirely isn't as easy as it sounds, especially in times like these and the world we're living in right now. It's more facile to break someone's trust and betray them rather than being an angel and keeping their secrets. The most significant quality one can look for in a partner is how much they value our trust. If you are confident that your partner will always have your back and you can be weak and vulnerable in front of them, maybe you should consider taking the next step. If you have told something to them in confidence and they don't share the information with anyone, and likewise if you do the same, then you both are fortunate. You should never break your partner's trust and expect the same from them.

2. **You support each other through the good and bad:**

Having someone by your side who you know would always support you, no matter what is nothing short of a blessing. Your partner has always comforted and consoled you through the negative phases and cherished and cheered you through the positive ones. Even if they were dealing with their problems, they made sure you were okay first. People like these are very hard to find. Most of the time, we tend to emotionally drain out or become frustrated by being there for people. But with your partner, you are always ready to lend a helping hand and even an ear, listen to all of their problems and shortcomings and support them every step of the way.

3. You both apologize to each other when needed:

One of the major signs of a toxic relationship is when your partner doesn't apologize or take accountability, even if they know they are wrong. These relationships tend to have a dead end. You might have noticed that your partner admits when wrong and apologizes, even if not straight away; they do it sooner or later. They try to sort out the arguments and fights calmly and try to listen to your point of views and opinions too, instead of forcing theirs on you. They make sure that you're okay after the fight and may even make small gestures to make you feel that they are guilty and you are more important than any of the arguments you both get into. Similarly, you do the same for them. This is an excellent sign that you should definitely step up your relationship to the next level.

4. You give each other space:

You both have a level of freedom and independence both within and outside the relationship. You both aren't on each other's throat and nerves every second. You both have different hobbies and passions that you pursue. You both can meet your friends alone or hang out by yourself, without stressing over if your partner would mind. This is a sign of a healthy relationship when you don't keep buzzing your partner with unlimited calls or texts, ask them about their whereabouts, or cling to them all day. Everyone deserves some free time of their own in which they can be alone and ponder over things.

5. You're on the same page with them:

Even if you and your partner don't share the same goals, hobbies, dreams, passions, or even the same views and opinions, you're still on the same page with them about your values and future. For example, both of you have discussed either having children or no children in the future, getting a destination wedding or a simple one, moving out of the city or across the country, or settling in the same spot where you both are right now. Agreeing on the same stuff shows that you both prioritize the same things and are compatible with stepping up your relationship.

6. You feel safe with them:

One of the signs that your relationship is ready for the next step is the feeling of comfort and security when you are with them. You can be your utter authentic self with them without fearing that they might judge you or dislike you. You have shown all of your sides to them, the good and the bad, and they still love you regardless. They like your quirks and don't get annoyed or irritated by your behavior. You also have accepted your partner's flaws and imperfections and still look at them the same way.

7. Your family and friends love them:

You have introduced them to your family as well as your friends. You were nervous at first as to if they will like them or not. But your partner turned out to be the charmer and swept your family members as well as your close friends off of their feet. They can't help but ask about your partner the minute you visit them and even tease you about taking the next big step with them. They have started to invite your partner on all the occasions and events to spend more time with them and get to know them better. All in all, your family and friends love your partner, and your partner's friends and family do the same to you.

Conclusion:

Taking the next big step in a relationship could be confusing and stressful, especially when you find yourself confused and unclear. But if you want to keep someone in your life forever, you have to make sure you make all the efforts to keep yourself with them. So if you have found someone worthy of your time and energy, don't let them go. Instead, cling onto them, and make efforts to keep your relationship floating.

Chapter 7:
6 Signs You Need To Give Your Partner Some Space

Intro:

We need a healthy amount of time alone to refresh, reflect on some things, de-stress and reset. But if you are in a relationship, and especially if you are living with them, it can be difficult to get the time you need. That is why it is really important to notice your partner's behaviour and see if they need that time alone. It is also important to talk about these frequently if you do not want to just keep guessing, but that can be difficult for some people. So we are listing some of the signs that will help you realize that your partner needs some space.

1. **They are nowhere to be found:**

If you have been noticing your partner sulking in another room or spending more time in front of the screen or are often found in their den or garage any place where you are normally not present, the reason could be that they need some time on their own. Of course, you will be tempted to go and see what they are doing there, but it would be best if you would leave them on their own this does not mean that they are tired of you or do not care. It just simply means they need space, and you should be considerate enough to give them that.

2. You have been arguing more often:

When people are tired, they tend to get annoyed at small things. Arguments are also one of the side effects of needing something and not getting it, which would be alone time. Unexplained irritation can be one of the biggest sign that your partner needs some time on their own to work on their issues, and it is not necessary that the issue has something to do with you. It is respectful to give them the time they need, which will also help flourish your relationship.

3. They aren't texting as frequently:

If your partner needs to sit back and take some time to reflect, they might not be as responsive to your messages as they usually are. It can be a way of protecting their alone time and directing their energy to themselves, and that is perfectly fine if your partner is still making an effort to reply to you even if less frequently you should ask them whether they need some time on their own it will also make them feel good.

4. They are giving you silent treatment:

The silent treatment is an immature response to things, but when people reach their breaking point, this the only thing that they think of as doable. So if your partner's needs haven't been met in quite some time, Them shutting down shouldn't come as a surprise. On the other hand, there are people who will not ask for space until they are at a fever pitch now. This can result in a person who needs the space feeling suffocated all the time, and there can also be frequent panic attacks. Of course, the solution to this is, respecting their boundaries even if they have not verbally asked for space, realizing that they need it. At the same time, you should also be working towards having better communication in your relationship.

5. They Keep cancelling plans:

Another big sign is cancelling plans without reason or giving a very lame excuse. When you are making plans without them, and they do not try to include themselves and just say things like, "you will have more fun without me" or "that's not really my thing", there is a huge chance they are just looking for a room to breathe. Although it is not a mature way to deal with things, it does make a point that I need some time on my own.

6. They seem closed off emotionally:

As we have mentioned before that if if your partner is removing him or herself from the room, that is a sign, but another thing you might notice is the emotional distance they will be less present in the relationship. If you see them being emotionally distant, you should sit with them and talk about it as this can be a reason for something other than needing space as well, and you do not want to play a guessing game and worsen things.

Conclusion:

You should be able to read the room so you can see what your partner needs, but this should not be the case all the time. Engaging in a healthy dialogue is very important, and that should be a practice in a healthy relationship. If you want your relationship to flourish, you should set boundaries and give each other the space you need so you both can grow in this relationship as well as individually.

Chapter 8:
5 Steps To Use Dating Apps Correctly

There's an old saying that goes like, "You have to kiss a lot of frogs first to find a prince," and these days, it applies to online dating. Does online dating feel like an unsolvable puzzle in your quest for finding 'the one" (or whoever it is that you're looking for)? Then worry no more because you're not alone in this. Online dating is an entirely different ballgame from meeting someone in real life. You have all the information you can get your hands on before meeting them. You may have gone through their short profile or may have exchanged a few words via text or email.

All in all, when you meet someone offline, you may have a lot or very little information about that person ahead of time. As they say, the first impression is the last impression; you have to make sure you apply it both in your online and offline life. Here are some ways to use dating apps correctly.

1. **Choose Your Photos Wisely**

As I've said before, that first impression matters, and nothing can make a better dating profile impression than putting up a great photo. Before setting up your profile, take your time to go through the shots that show off your looks and hint at how your personality is. It would be best if you also kept in mind to post some well establishing shots that your match can use to recognize you when you finally meet them in person. Choose one picture of your close-up face and one more distant snap that shows a complete view of your body. Your features should be visible and don't even think to use an old photo to trick your potential match. We might not be the best judge of our faces, so make sure to ask one or two of your close friends about the pictures you are choosing.

2. Work On Your Bio

A picture may be worth a thousand words, but the bio of your profile is still essential. Even if you are the most charming and loveliest person globally, a blank or a terrible bio will get you nowhere with the people using the apps. Some apps give you enough space to write a complete autobiography, while some limit you to a line or two. No matter what limit or space you get, look deep into yourself and start thinking about your personality and traits that make you different from other people. You should be careful about the areas you should avoid and the ones you should enhance in your profile.

3. Expand Your Expectations

Once you have created a fantastic profile, start looking for partners. Don't be too picky considering the overwhelming number of people using the apps; the possibilities can distract you from the great profiles that are right in front of you. It's normal to find a chance with someone you hadn't considered initially, and it's crucial to venture outside your dating comfort zone. While you should look out for someone with the same opinions and personality as yourself, you shouldn't restrict your options. If you haven't had any luck finding a good match, it may be time to broaden your search terms ad change your criteria. A little flexibility wouldn't do you any harm.

4. **Remain Active**

You may find yourself getting bored after using the apps for an extensive period. However, it is essential to keep your profile up to date, remember to log in regularly, send messages and run searches, even if you aren't looking for love at the moment. Some algorithms determine what appears on your social apps. So, with every action you take on an app or site, it reveals your preferences and allows you to receive more likely matches. Similarly, if you fail to check the app regularly, it will stop sending the appropriate profiles your way.

5. **Make The First Move**

If you potentially get your match and hang out with them, make the first move and ask them out. No matter if it's the guy or the girl, if your intentions are clear about the other person, then it shouldn't stop you both from seeing each other. Ask for their schedule and plan a date whenever they're available. Make them feel comfortable first and get them to trust you so they can go out with you without any hesitation.

Conclusion

Bring the fun element into dating apps, and don't just make it seem like you're doing some work. Be patient because things like these take time. Keep engaging and stay positive; you might now meet someone instantly. Explore your options and then hope for the best. If you need to take a break, do it, and then come back when you're ready to dive in again.

Chapter 9:
7 Ways To Become A Good Partner

Intro:

All relationships are unique. Different Experiences, personalities, interests, beliefs and culture tell us about the possibility of hundreds of different types of couples. However, some foundational qualities assure us of a lasting and healthy relationship no matter what kind of two people are involved. Whether you are in a relationship right now or you are single, you know what works for you, and you might be neglecting without even giving it a second thought. So, right now, what you should do is sit back, relax and think about what worked for you and what did not in your past relationships and what was lacking. You can also ask the people around you who are in committed relationships and what worked for them. Although the relationship dynamics of everyone are different, there is always something to learn. We are going to tell you a secret here. For a healthy and long-lasting relationship, you need to work on yourself first. We are going to list down 7 ways in which you can become a good partner.

1. Be Secure Within Yourself:

So often in your twenties, you feel like you are ready for a lasting relationship, but around that time, most people have not figured out what their passions are, or they are not confident enough. If you still have not figured out your outlet through which you will contribute to the world, and you are trying to lay the foundation of a new relationship, new home, chances are your relationship will not last long because you will feel restless all the time. However, once you have figured out your sense of being, it brings you a sense of contentment. It will be easier for you to maintain the balance between your work and your relationship. If you are secure with who you are, people's comments or words will not be able to bring you down. That can be difficult for people for various reasons, but you will have a happy relationship once you can do it.

2. Be Responsible:

You are going to have good days and bad days. There are going to be days where you will wake up sad and grumpy. After the emotion subsides, you should ask yourself what could be the reason for this. You should always take the responsibility of seeing the truth behind your emotion. Was it your partner's behaviour that made you feel left out or like a third wheel? Tell them. If you feel like your partner is taking advantage of your efforts and are working for this relationship as much as you do, talk to them about this. When you are in a relationship like this, these conversations are not always easy, but you need them to create a stronger bond.

3. Be Appreciative:

If you show appreciation for little things, it will strengthen your relationship. It could be as simple as calling them and letting them know when will you be home, making dinner or putting the garbage on the curb. All these little things show that you appreciate their existence in your life and are considerate of their time and feelings.

4. Laugh Together:

When you laugh as a couple, you open yourself up to your partner; this allows you to be vulnerable. When you can laugh at yourself and themselves in each other's presence, it will build trust towards each other that they will not judge, humiliate or capitalize but rather enjoy these small moments with you.

5. Spend Quality Time Together:

If you treat the relationship in your life as a priority, you will want to spend time together. Of course, there will be times when you will be socializing with others, but that will not give you moments of intimacy or bonding. Instead, you need to take time out to be together. You can have dinner at your favourite restaurant, watch a movie, cook dinner together, go hiking or just simply stay at home and watch Netflix and chill.

6. Be Their Number One Fan:

All of us can achieve amazing things in life, but when our loved ones appreciate us, it gives us a confidence boost when the people we love are standing behind us, supporting us as we work towards our goals. So as a partner, you need to understand your partner's dreams and goals and support them as they strive to achieve their goals, in good times and bad. You should let them know that you are always going to stand with them. When you know you have your partner's support, it is the best feeling in the world. But always remember, it is a two-way street.

7. Be a Good Listen and Observer:

Suppose you want to be a good partner. In that case, you must understand what annoys them. To do that, you should pay close attention to what they are saying. You need to listen to them and understand what makes them happy, what upsets them, but simultaneously you should be observing how they react in certain situations. What makes them nervous, and what makes them comfortable. You will get to know more about them by observing.

Conclusion:

We listed how you can be a better partner and make your special feel loved, but you should always remember that a relationship is a two-way street, and they should be putting in the same amount of effort. Make sure that your partner has not become lazy in love, and if you think one of you is getting there, you should have some activities that can bring things back on track, but you and your partner should have a mutual understanding.

www.ingramcontent.com/pod-product-compliance
Lightning Source LLC
Chambersburg PA
CBHW071526080526
44588CB00011B/1566